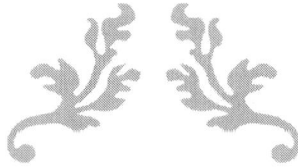

APPRENTICESHIPS

A GUIDE FOR STUDENTS AND PARENTS

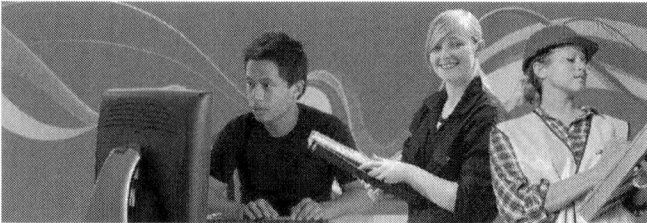

Louise Webber

Copyright © 2018 Louise Webber

All rights reserved.

DEDICATION

This book is dedicated to the apprenticeship students and employers I have worked with over the years, for their hard work, support and determination.

CONTENTS

1   Introduction

2   History of Apprenticeships

3   Statistics about Apprenticeships

4   Becoming an Apprentice

5   Why an Apprenticeship?

6   Famous former Apprentices

7   Getting an Apprenticeship job

8   The recruitment process

9   Initial assessments

10 Creating your CV

11 How much will I earn?

12 Levels of Apprenticeships

13 Student discounts

14 What is the 20% off-the-job training rule?

15 What happens if I leave my employer?

16 Safeguarding learners

17 Physical, emotional and mental well-being of Apprentices

18 The review process

19 What is the likelihood of you successfully completing your Apprenticeship?

20   Apprenticeship frameworks

21   Apprenticeship standards

22   E-portfolio systems and paper folders

23   Gathering evidence for your portfolio

24   The Apprenticeship Levy and Government funding

25   End point assessments (EPA)

26   What does the end-point assessment involve?

27   Roles and responsibilities within Apprenticeships

28   Induction and getting started on your course

29   Centre appeals procedures

30   Choosing a training provider

31   RoATP – Register of Apprenticeship Training Providers

32   The importance of OFSTED reports

33   Choosing an employer

34   Functional skills

35   Examples of functional skills requirements

36   What happens if I fail my functional skills tests?

37   Electronic support for functional skills test preparation

38   Functional skills examinations

39   National Apprenticeship Week

40   Case studies

41   Your Apprenticeship journey

42   Useful websites for further information

43   About the author

44   Acknowledgements

45   Disclaimer

46   First publishing date

47   Appendix 1: List of apprenticeship standards

1 INRODUCTION

Have you heard of the concept "Earn While You Learn"?

This is the basis of one of the UK Government advertising campaigns encouraging young people to apply for Apprenticeship job roles.

The idea of an Apprenticeship is to gain skills and knowledge whilst employed as an Apprentice and earning money. There are a wide array of Apprenticeship courses available in the UK, such as Business Administration, Management, Accountancy, Construction, Warehousing, Hairdressing, Health and Social Care and many, many more. Think of an industry and you can pretty much guarantee there is an Apprenticeship route available. In fact, Apprenticeships cover around 1500 roles.

There are even degree level Apprenticeships

available, which lead to a full university degree, but without the cost of tuition fees.

The Department for Business, Innovation and Skills state that around 90% of Apprentices stay employed after completing their Apprenticeship.

There are many statistics available to state that Apprentices can earn more money than graduates. Many successful people have started out on Apprenticeships and become very wealthy and had fantastic careers.

You will see statistics such as "Apprentices earn £100,000 more over their working life than graduates". I am not sure how true or accurate these figures are, and with so much contradictory information out there, I would not like to confirm the accuracy or otherwise. However, I can say with certainty that those that leave school to go into an Apprenticeship rather than go to university, will start earning sooner than a graduate, and with hard work, commitment and determination, the earnings of Apprentices are certainly not limited in the long term.

The other main consideration of an Apprenticeship compared with university is that there are no fees to pay, and Apprentices literally earn while they learn, so there is no massive student debt to repay at the end of the course.

A typical student on a three-year course outside of London might expect to graduate with around £35,000 to £40,000 of student loans, whilst an Apprentice will be earning money all the time, whilst still gaining qualifications. In addition, the Apprentice will be gaining work experience, which has been proven to be very valuable in career enhancement.

The upshot here is that if you have the ability to do a great job, work hard and show commitment to the company you work for, then you, as an Apprentice, are in a great position to gain full time employment, potential promotion and the financial benefits that accompany success.

Apprentices spend around 20% of their time studying during their working hours. Whilst university students are supposedly studying full time, in reality the structure of lectures and tutorials may mean that it is much less than that. From my own experience, in my last year of university, I had just two hours a week of lectures and the rest of the time was built around a few tutorials and self-study. If I had paid the typical £9000 in tuition fees, as is the standard these days, I would not really see that as value for money.

As a parent myself now, I want to see my children making the most of every moment to enhance their skills and knowledge. For me, value for money training and education is essential. I don't want my children to start their adult lives with heaps of debt and all the stress that goes with it.

There are many different levels of Apprenticeship, which are explored later in this book. Schemes last a minimum of one year and up to five or six years for some degree level Apprenticeships.

This book explores many aspects of Apprenticeships, how they work in practice and will help by giving support and advice to help on your Apprenticeship journey.

2 HISTORY OF APPRENTICESHIPS

The term Apprenticeship was first coined in the later middle ages, when master craftsmen employed young people as a form of inexpensive labour, and offered food, accommodation and training in their craft in return for hard work.

Most Apprentices, at that time were very young, starting around the age of 10-15 years old. This was clearly open to exploitation and often Apprentices were ill-treated, over worked and under-rewarded. Most Apprentices worked for their master for a term of 7 years, with the hope of one day becoming a master-craftsman themselves, but for the majority this ambition was never fully realised.

Today however, Apprenticeships are heavily regulated with a focus on 'outcomes for learners'.

This regulation means that training providers or colleges who support Apprenticeship schemes will be supporting the best interests of the Apprentice. This also ensures that employers treat Apprentices ethically and really do develop their skills and knowledge. These days it is all about the statistics, and the statistics show that most Apprentices are successful and stay employed, with many going on to promotion, increased salaries and further opportunities.

'Outcomes for Learners' is a key driver for training providers, who are keen to see Apprentices succeed. Government funding means Government regulation and a focus on results. That's great news for you as an Apprentice, because the Government - and your training provider - will want you to succeed.

In 2008 the Government published a document called 'Strategy for Future Apprenticeships in England' and following it, the National Apprenticeship Service was launched in 2009, with the aim to bring about growth in the number of employers offering Apprenticeships.

Prior to this the Government were keen to increase the number of young people attending university, aiming to get as many as 50% of 18-year old's into higher education through this route.

However, many European countries were more focused on Apprenticeships and this was beginning to seem like a positive way of educating young people. It was then reported that the earning potential of Apprentices was actually greater than that of many university students.

A university degree is often said to vastly improve earning potential, but it was found that this was highly dependent on the choice of degree and many university graduates were unemployed or worked in industries unrelated to their qualification.

Recent reports have shown that Apprentices earnings can surpass that of university graduates by up to 270%. This rebukes many of the common misconceptions about Apprenticeships and uptake on Apprenticeships has more than doubled over the past decade.

With massive financial pressures on university graduates, due to the abolition of grants and the introduction of tuition fees, university can become an unrealistic option for many. Apprentices can start work at an earlier age. With earlier earning potential can come a fast track route for home ownership or buying a car. Apprenticeships are now far more highly regarded as a viable and valuable career path and a genuine and comparable alternative to university, which even a decade ago was not fully appreciated.

All this is great news for you as an Apprentice. With increased regulation and strong Government backing, Apprenticeships really do offer a great foot up the career ladder, whether it be a first job role or a development opportunity within a company you already work for.

3 STATISTICS ABOUT APPRENTICESHIPS

The Government (ESFA) published the following information in 2017 relating to Apprenticeships:

Number of Apprenticeship Starts in 2016-2017	491,300
Average number of Apprenticeship opportunities listed on the find an Apprenticeship website	23,000
Degree level Apprenticeship starts 2016-2017	1670
Percentage of Apprentices under the age of 19 in 2016 - 2017	24.6%
The number of online Apprenticeship applications made in 2015-2016	1,656,630
The percentage of Apprentices who felt that their ability to do their job had improved	97%

The percentage of Apprentices who go into work or further training	90%
The percentage of Apprentices who felt their Apprenticeship had a positive impact on their career	92%
The percentage of employers who said they were satisfied with the programme	87%
The amount that higher Apprentices could earn on average over their lifetime compared to those with level 3 vocational qualifications	£150,000

Source:

https://www.gov.uk/government/publications/key-facts-about-apprenticeships/key-facts-about-apprenticeships

4 BECOMING AN APPRENTICE

You can apply for an apprenticeship while you're still at school. To start one, you'll need to be:

- 16 or over by the end of the summer holidays
- living in England
- not in full-time education
- There is no longer an upper age limit

You do not need to be a school leaver to become an apprentice. You can become an apprentice at any age. Many apprentices are young adults, but there are also apprentices who have been working for some time and wish to enhance their skills and knowledge. You can even stay with your existing employer, and 'up-skill' through an Apprenticeship.

5 WHY AN APPRENTICESHIP?

Apprenticeships represent a fantastic opportunity for you to develop skills and knowledge whilst earning a wage.

The main advantages of apprenticeships:

- Earning a salary/wage
- Holiday and sick pay entitlements
- No debt from tuition fees
- Free training and tutor support
- Clear targets and progression opportunities
- A contract of employment
- Learning at a pace that suits you
- Gain nationally recognised qualifications
- Work on several qualifications at the same time (e.g. maths, English, ICT, Btec, NVQ)
- Support from a Training Provider or College
- Most Apprentices remain in employment
- Most Apprentices report taking on additional responsibility, promotion and/or pay increases by the end of their course
- You could even be given a pay rise (and yes, even when you are still on your Apprenticeship)

- You could even be promoted (again, yes, even when you are still on your Apprenticeship)
- Your employer may have invested money (through the Levy) and so will be more likely to invested in your future
- It is reported that those on higher level Apprenticeships have earning potential of over £150,000 more than graduates over their working lifetime

6 FAMOUS FORMER APPRENTICES

Some of the countries' most prominent and successful figures and entrepreneurs started out as Apprentices.

Apprentices make an essential contribution to our economy, boosting productivity and developing the skills and knowledge of our workforce to achieve great things. Apprenticeships are set to deliver £100BN to the UK economy by 2050.

Here is a brief list of famous former Apprentices, many of whom you may see on so called "rich lists"

- **Michael Caine:** apprentice plumber who became an actor.
- **Gordon Ramsay:** former catering Apprentice, now celebrity chef and television star
- **Jamie Oliver:** former catering Apprentice, now celebrity chef and television star
- **John Caudwell:** former engineering Apprentice who founded Phones4U
- **John Frieda:** former apprentice hairdresser

- **David Beckham:** formerly on a Youth Training Scheme became England footballer
- **Billy Connolly:** apprentice welder who became a comedian and actor.
- **Sir Alex Ferguson:** shipyard apprentice who went on to become the Manchester United manager.
- **Charlie Mullins:** apprentice plumber who now owns Pimlico Plumbers
- **Anthony Bamford:** Chairman of JCB
- **Ross Brawn:** Formula 1 Managing Director of Motorsports
- **Stewart Wingate:** Chief Executive London Gatwick Airport
- **Clare Smyth:** Chef with three Michelin Stars

7 GETTING AN APPRENTICESHIP JOB

Apprenticeship jobs *can* be hard to come by. For some jobs advertised at our centre, we get up to 200 applications for just one job. This doesn't mean that *you* can't be successful.

Some industries are easier to get into than others. You need to make sure that your application looks as good as it possibly can be and that you give the best possible impression of yourself that you can at every stage of the application process.

As a business manager for the past 20 plus years, I have been heavily involved in the recruitment of new staff into my businesses. From an employer's point of view, the most important things to be considered when hiring a potential recruit are:

- A positive attitude to your career and learning
- A dependable approach
- Enthusiasm
- Hard working and committed to the company

It is important to show the recruiter that you really

want the job and that you will add value to their business.

At any one time there are up to 28,000 Apprenticeship vacancies available online across a variety of industries or trades.

You can visit Gov.uk and search for 'apprenticeships'. You can then look by keyword and/or location. If you find a vacancy you might be interested in you can then register on the website and follow the online instructions to apply for the job.

You can also look on the following website: nationalcareerservice.direct.gov.uk

Or call an adviser on 0800 100 900 which is free from landlines and mobiles.

Vacancies can also be found on the following websites:

- National Apprenticeship Service
- Ucas Careerfinder
- Find an Apprenticeship
- All about School Leavers
- Not going to uni
- Milkround School Leavers

There are many other ways of finding an

Apprenticeship.

Many training providers will advertise vacancies on their own social media pages. It is worthwhile researching local Apprenticeship training providers to find out their names and follow their pages. In addition, you will find 'apps' for your phone for some training providers who also share job vacancies this way. Have a look in the 'app store'.

You can also 'follow' companies that you may wish to work with on social media. Some companies post vacancy information this way too. Social media can also give you more of an insight into the company, so you get a feel for their values and culture.

Look out for careers events and spend some time on the National Apprenticeship Service website. It is worth doing this early on so that you don't miss opportunities.

If you are thinking of applying for an Apprenticeship after leaving school, you might want to consider asking your parents or other adults to follow these pages too and you can start researching as early as Year 11 or 12 to gain a good insight into what you want.

8 THE RECRUITMENT PROCESS

The recruitment process of some firms can be fairly similar to that of graduate recruitment.

This could include:

- Initial telephone interview
- Online assessment tests
- Presentations
- Online interviews
- Structured assessment days
- Formal interviews
- Panel interviews

Not all companies will be so formal. Many require you to come in for an informal chat first to see if you feel the job is right for you and they feel that you might have the potential they are looking for. Don't forget though that every interaction with a potential employer is a chance to show them what you are capable of.

Some employers might offer you a position after just one informal interview, others may ask for you to complete a work trial. It really does depend on the company and what they are looking for.

It is really important that you do some research into the company before meeting with them. It is now very easy to look online and find out about a company. Social media is also a great place to start. If a candidate came to see me for a job and knew nothing about the company, I would be disappointed.

I know this sounds basic, but I cannot state enough that first impressions matter and, whilst it would be nice if society judged people purely on their personality, the reality is that you need to look the part as well. If you turn up for your interview for an office job in your joggers, you will have to work really hard to convince them you'll be great at the job and to overcome initial impressions. That said if you are looking at a painting and decorating Apprenticeship, it may be inappropriate to go in a suit, but maybe something a bit more smart-casual.

Be careful about what you put on social media when you are looking for work. Many employers will look on your LinkedIn or Facebook pages to gain an idea of what you are really like. If you don't think your Facebook page shows you at your best to a potential employer, it might be worth increasing your privacy settings.

9 INITIAL ASSESSMENTS

When you first apply for an Apprenticeship you may be asked to complete initial assessments. This is a requirement of funded Apprenticeships.

Initial assessments are usually done online (on such systems such as BKSB) or can be paper-based. Apprentices often get confused and think these are exams, but they are simply an assessment of where you are with your functional skills.

Your initial assessment tests will cover maths and English. For some courses you may also be required to take an ICT assessment.

You may be sent the initial assessment details to login to a system remotely. It is very important that you complete the initial assessment under test conditions. The score you get may affect the level of work you are later asked to do. The accuracy of the score you get is very important so that your tutor knows how to help you and what support you will need. You may however need to reach a certain standard in order to progress with the course you want (this is up to the training provider to decide), but training providers will look at your overall application when considering you for an Apprenticeship role.

10 CREATING YOUR CV

Your CV is a very important document that will summarise your work experience, skills and qualifications to showcase you to potential employers and training providers.

As this is often the *very* first thing a potential employer will see about you, it is well worth making the effort to ensure it is as good as it possibly can be. It is your chance to show off and the more you showcase your skills or potential the better your chances of success.

There are lots of online resources and templates to help you create a CV. It needs to be professionally produced, clear, concise and easy to read. Have a look online to see top tips for producing an excellent CV. Some training providers will help you to improve your CV before sending it forward to a potential employer. It is a good idea to ask the training provider or recruitment consultant what they think of your CV and if you could make any improvements. It costs nothing to ask and it may well help you land that dream job.

Your CV should contain the following:

- Your name
- Your address
- Telephone number
- Email address
- If you have a driving licence
- A brief profile about you, what you have done and what you are looking to do
- Your career history
- Your academic history and qualifications
- Professional qualifications if you have any
- Personal achievements, interesting things you have done/hobbies
- You can also add the details of two references (or you can simply write 'references available upon request').

Try to keep your CV to less than 2 pages if you can. It should be professionally produced, so avoid fancy font types. There is debate about whether to include a photo or not. This is pretty much a matter of opinion, but if in doubt, it is probably best avoided. If you do include a photo, ensure that it is a professional looking headshot photo.

11 HOW MUCH WILL I EARN?

The minimum wage for apprentices is £3.70 per hour*, but many employers pay more than this.

This is dependent on the sector, region and apprenticeship level e.g. some higher apprenticeships pay up to £500 per week.

The minimum wage for Apprentices is for those under the age of 19 and those aged 19 and over who are in their first year.

> **Example:** An apprentice aged 22 in the first year of their apprenticeship is entitled to a minimum hourly rate of £3.70

You must be paid at least the minimum wage rate for your age if you are employed as an Apprentice and you are over 19 years of age AND have completed your first year.

Example: An apprentice aged 22 who has completed the first year of their apprenticeship is entitled to a minimum hourly rate of £7.38

You must be paid for your normal working hours (as outlined in your contract of employment) and training that is part of your Apprenticeship.

Apprentices who started their courses after 1st May 2017 must have at least 20% of their working time as 'off the job training'.

In addition, you will be entitled to 20 days paid holiday per year as well as bank holidays (pro-rata dependent on hours).

Your employer **is permitted to pay you more** than the rates above. They do not have to pay you just the minimum wage, but can pay more if they wish.

*Minimum wage details correct at the time this book was last updated (in May 2018).

You can check for up to date information on wages and benefits at the website below:

https://www.gov.uk/apprenticeships-guide/pay-and-conditions

12 LEVELS OF APPRENTICESHIP

Apprenticeships have equivalent educational levels.

Name	Level	Equivalent educational level
Intermediate	2	GCSE
Advanced	3	A 'level
Higher	4, 5, 6, 7	Foundation degree and above
Degree	6 and 7	Bachelors or master's degree

You might look at this and think that level 2 seems quite low if you have already achieved your GCSEs or A Levels.

However, most first time Apprenticeship roles will start at Level 2. This is because the Apprentice will (generally) have little or no experience in the industry in which they will be working.

The qualifications obtained throughout the Apprenticeship course are work-based qualifications. This means that learners need to demonstrate sufficient skills (as well as knowledge) to achieve the qualification, and usually this is through demonstration of practical work skills.

There is a substantial 'jump' in work levels and requirements between the levels.

At level 2 learners are expected to show a basic understanding of concepts and basic skills. At level 3 learners will generally be looking at a deeper understanding and by levels 4 and 5, learners will be producing work that is much more analytical (and hold job roles with substantial levels of responsibility).

Whilst there are always comparisons to be made to GCSE and A 'Level, in reality, these are a very different sort of qualification and show different skills to GCSE and A 'Level. As an employer, when I am looking to recruit new staff, I look for a range of skills, as well as academic ability or potential, so a candidate with both academic and work-based qualifications, along with good communication skills would certainly be a positive consideration for a suitable role.

Even if you have a degree, you may still qualify to become an Apprentice, but this will depend on the funding rules that apply, which can change, so it is always worth asking.

What you will need to demonstrate to the apprenticeship funder is that you will be gaining sufficient, additional skills and knowledge that justify Government funding. For example, you may have a degree in history, but have decided this is not for you, and you wish to become a carpenter and therefore need to re-train. You may then need to start at Level 2 as you have no prior knowledge or skills in this industry.

Many learners on Higher Level Apprenticeships are already in a job role, but see Apprenticeships as an opportunity to develop further and add additional skills and knowledge to progress their career. This provides opportunities for adult learners to progress and through the Apprenticeship scheme gain support from their employer and the training centre or college they are affiliated to.

13 STUDENT DISCOUNTS

As an Apprentice you can apply for a student discount card.

These student cards offer similar discounts to those you would get if you were a university student.

The NUS Apprentice Extra card offers discounts for UK Apprentices. There are lots of discounts available online and in store for shopping as well as travel and restaurant discounts available.

Your training provider should have leaflets or details about the discounts available for their students.

Try the NUS Apprentice Extra website for details. The card costs around £11 for 12 months*.

https://www.apprenticeextra.co.uk/

*Price correct as of date of publishing.

You can also download APPs such as Student Beans, which will give you great discounts too. Amazon Prime Student is also available to Apprentices who have an NUS Apprentice Extra card. More mature apprentices are eligible for NUS Apprentice Extra cards too.

14 WHAT IS THE 20% OFF THE JOB TRAINING RULE?

The importance of quality training and support for Apprentices has been long established.

Ofsted have pin-pointed quality off-the-job training as an essential feature of a quality Apprenticeship and this was also evidenced as part of the Richard Review back in 2012.

Therefore, strict guidelines have now been put in place to ensure that this time is allocated to learners. 20% of Apprentices' time at work should be spent doing off-the-job training during an Apprenticeship. This is the same for both Apprenticeship Frameworks and Apprenticeship Standards.

To make the time calculations simple: If you work as an Apprentice for 5 days a week, then 1 day of the 5, should be spent on off-the-job training. You do not have to have this time in one block, or all on one day, as long as it adds up over the entirety of your course.

It is the responsibility of the training provider/college and the employer to ensure this time is allocated, as described in the funding rules.

Off-the-job training must be:

- Directly relevant to the Apprenticeship Framework or Standard

And can include activities such as:

- Training workshops
- Lectures
- Role playing
- Simulation exercises
- E-learning
- Shadowing
- Mentoring
- Industry visits
- Research and reading – including online research
- Attendance at competitions
- Learning support sessions
- Time spent on assignments
- Time spent completing assessments

Off-the-job training does not include English and maths up to level 2 as this is funded separately. It also does not include progress reviews or on-programme assessment needed for an Apprenticeship Framework or Standard. In addition, it cannot include training which takes place outside the apprentice's paid working hours.

Off-the-job training can take place at the

Apprentices' place of work or at a training centre or college.

Training providers or colleges will normally have some way of recording your off-the-job training hours. This might be a log or learning diary. It is important that you keep this log up to date as it may be required for inspection.

Make the most of this learning log if you are given one, as it will be a useful reflective learning tool for you. I would recommend that you keep your learning log or learning diary close to hand at all times. That way, you can make notes as and when training occurs, as it can be difficult to remember exactly what training has occurred later.

Full details of the 20% off-the-job training rules can be found at the website below:

https://www.gov.uk/government/uploads/system/uploads/attachment_data/file/621565/OTJ_training_guidance.pdf

15 WHAT HAPPENS IF I LEAVE MY EMPLOYER?

Training centres and Colleges invest a lot of time and effort to create alliances with employers. They will want you to stay with your employer if you possibly can. It certainly looks good on your CV if you can show that you have completed what you started, and a CV showing you moving from job to job does not give potential future employers a good first impression.

I would always recommend you stick it out with your employer if you can. From my own experience within a training centre, I know how hard it is to find good placements with good employers. Not only that, a good training centre, that has been running Apprenticeship courses for some time, will phase out working with employers who get poor feedback from learners. So then, in theory at least, most of the employers should be positive and supportive, or centres simply won't want to place their candidates with them.

However, there will be times when Apprentices feel they cannot remain at the place of employment. This could be due to personal circumstances, such as moving to a new house. It could be that the

Apprentice is not enjoying the atmosphere at work or has a personality clash or other issues with another member of staff. There are many reasons why an Apprentice may want to leave work or feels they have to.

Whatever the circumstances, don't give up hope. You MAY still be able to finish your Apprenticeship course and still gain those all-important qualifications.

The important thing to remember is that you need to communicate with your training provider or college. It is best, when possible, to talk issues through with your personal tutor, or other support staff, prior to leaving. It is not a good idea to just leave, or resign, unless of course you feel unsafe for any reason.

You may find that issues can be resolved and that you may actually be okay to stay at work once these have been ironed out.

If the situation is not rectifiable and you need to leave work, then your training provider or college may be able to find another suitable placement for you. Obviously, you will need to go through interviews again, but don't forget the centre know you now, and this could be a great advantage at getting a new placement if you have worked hard so far and been reliable. You may need to have a 'break in learning' while you are out of work, and so this may extend the completion date of your course, but this would need to be approved by your funder.

If you have found yourself a new job, then you might still be able to complete your Apprenticeship. Provided that the new job role provides suitable opportunities for you to provide the evidence and training opportunities needed for your course, you can talk to your training provider and see if you can make arrangements to continue training. The centre will have lots of paperwork to do to organise the transfer of employer, but they should be happy to do this as long as your new employer is happy and the job suits the course. The training centre will need to complete a Health and Safety check with the new company and obtain approval from them to agree to continue your training.

Your training centre or college will have to check that you still meet funding rules in order to continue and there may be issues if your Apprenticeship has been funded by your employer.

The upshot here is that it is always worth checking to see if you can continue.

Your qualifications will be a valuable enhancement to your CV. Don't give them up easily.

16 SAFEGUARDING LEARNERS

Training providers and colleges have a duty of care to ensure learners are safe.

From a Health and Safety perspective, this includes inspecting employers' premises to ensure Health and Safety compliance, so that you will be working in safe physical environment.

The training provider or college will keep documented reports to show that they have inspected the place of employment, normally once a year.

In addition, the training provider will obtain a copy of the Employers Liability Insurance Certificate. This is an important document which proves that the company that you will be working for as an Apprentice is sufficiently covered if there is an accident at the workplace. It is the law that all employers have this insurance.

Useful Website: https://www.gov.uk/employers-liability-insurance

The centre or college will have a safeguarding officer, who you can contact if you have any other concerns, such as work-place bullying or harassment issues. Make sure you know who they are and how to contact them if you need any support.

17 PHYSICAL, EMOTIONAL, AND MENTAL WELL-BEING OF APPRENTICES

In addition to job specific training, training providers will look to support and educate Apprentices in respect of their physical, emotional and mental well-being. A good training provider will have resources available for learners to support this, such as a Health and Wellbeing area within their E-portfolio resources, leaflets available to students who attend on site or hold specialist sessions to cover wellbeing.

All training providers and colleges (as well as schools) have a legal obligation to teach British Values and the government have strengthened guidance on improving the spiritual, moral, social and cultural development of students. The Government state that training providers have "a duty to actively promote the fundamental British Values of democracy, the rule of law, individual liberty and mutual respect and tolerance" as set out by the government in the 'Prevent' strategy in 2011.

This means that learners will benefit from additional training in addition to the basic course requirements. A good training provider or college will relate this information well to the learner's own experiences and place of work, to enhance their understanding of their job role as well as wider issues such as anti-terrorism. For example, if you are a Team Leading Apprentice, a session may revolve around how to manage conflict at work. This enhances Apprentices wider understanding of society and how to deal with wider issues.

Part of the review process (which is normally around every 8 – 10 weeks) Apprentices are also supported with discussions around Health and Safety, British Values and Safeguarding. This is to ensure the Apprentice feels safe, is well supported at work and develops knowledge and understanding of the world around them, as well as relevant issues in the news. Ofsted expect to see evidence of this work and so training providers should be working hard to embed this into learning sessions for Apprentices.

Useful Website:
https://www.gov.uk/government/news/guidance-on-promoting-british-values-in-schools-published

18 THE REVIEW PROCESS

Around about every 8-10 weeks (absolute max. 12 weeks) you will have a formal review meeting with your personal tutor. This is a great opportunity for you and you should make the most of the time you have 1:1 together.

During the meeting you will complete a formal review form. The form helps you and your tutor to review your progress together and set targets for work for you to complete by your next review or meeting. You and your tutor should agree SMART targets (Specific, Measurable, Attainable, Realistic and Timely).

You should be very clear of what expectations your tutor has of you. Your employer will also be involved in the review meeting so you should make good use of this time to ensure your employer is happy with your progress at work and if you need to make any adjustments to your way of working or improve your performance. Your employer will complete a section of the review form to document your performance so far. Make the most of the feedback given to you during these meetings, the best Apprentices learn from their mistakes and from other people they work with.

I worked with an Apprentice once who was lucky enough to get a role within a successful IT company. IT Apprenticeships can be hard to get and he really impressed at interview. He was delighted to get the job and learn a new trade in this dynamic industry.

During his first review the employer told me (in private) that he was spoilt and lazy and was not pulling his weight. It seemed that the employer was looking to terminate the contract. Obviously, this is not something we want as a training provider and I wanted to support the Apprentice as much as possible.

As his tutor, I arranged a meeting between the three of us (tutor, Apprentice & employer) and it actually turned out that the Apprentice was unclear as to what to do and so was seemingly lazy, but was actually just totally confused so had been putting off tasks.

Between the three of us, we created an action plan, with clear goals for the Apprentice to work towards. Six months later, he was offered a pay rise and a promotion. This demonstrates the importance of good communication and the high level of support you should expect from your personal tutor.

If you do have any concerns, it is important that you talk to your tutor and make the most of the support that they can offer you.

During the review meeting your tutor will make it clear to you how far you have progressed on your course and what work you have left to complete.

19 WHAT IS THE LIKELYHOOD OF YOU SUCCESSFULLY COMPLETING YOUR APPRENTICESHIP?

Well in reality, this is pretty much down to you. You should have undergone a good level of assessment prior to acceptance on the course. This should have included some or all of the following:

- Initial assessment test for English and maths (some courses also require ICT)
- A telephone or face to face interview with the college or training provider
- An interview with your employer

In addition, you may also have been asked to:

- Complete personality/psychometric testing
- Complete initial assignments or assessments to verify the standard of your written work and/or understanding
- Complete a work trial

Of course, once you have passed all of that, in theory, the Apprenticeship should now be a breeze. If you are in the right job, with a supportive employer and a good personal tutor and you work hard, then really there is no reason you should not successfully complete the course.

Just to put this into perspective for you, training providers and colleges are targeted on success rates. This means that **they want you to pass**. They want to support you and have a vested interest in doing so.

Ofsted requirements are such that if success rates aren't good, then a training provider or college will struggle to get a good or outstanding report, which is important to them. If they don't get a good Ofsted rating their future funding contracts and employer contracts may be at risk and believe me that is the last thing they want.

It is worth asking your training provider to let you know what the success rate is on the course you are on. Many 'good' or 'outstanding' training providers will proudly advertise this information on notice boards or in their newsletters or on social media.

If you see that last year only 25% of people on a course like yours passed, you might want to at least question why that was. There may be a very good reason (for example the training provider may have had a large contract with an employer who went into liquidation).

If your training provider can show that around 75% or more of the Apprentices pass the course then this is around the national average for success rates. Even this means that three out of four won't compete, but in my experience, this is generally down to Apprentices personal circumstances (moving house, on the wrong course in the first place, lack of motivation etc.) rather than down to the training provider.

20 APPRENTICESHIP FRAMEWORKS

Many Apprenticeship Courses are based on Frameworks, which essentially means that you will work towards many qualifications at the same time.

This is great because you could end up with up to 10* certificates to add to your CV from one Apprenticeship course.

The Apprenticeship Frameworks generally consist of the following elements:

- COMPETENCE BASED QUALIFICATION – such as an NVQ (National Vocational Qualification) or SVQ (Scottish Vocational Qualification). Vocational qualifications aim to show learners occupational competence within their chosen job role

- KNOWLEDGE BASED QUALIFICATON – such as a Btec or City and Guilds qualification.

- EMPLOYEE RIGHTS AND RESPONSIBILITIES (ERR) – aims to teach learners about basic employment rights, industry structures and the impact on the sector of public law and policies

- FUNCTIONAL SKILLS – Maths and English. Some frameworks also require ICT

- PERSONAL LEARNING AND THINKING SKILLS – this is broken down into the following sections: Independent Enquiry, Creative Thinking, Reflective Learning, Self-Management and Effective Participation. Learners will reflect on how they have met the criteria for each section and evidence how they have met the criteria required through the other elements of the Apprenticeship, including work skills or Btec/NVQ work.

10 certificates:

Maths Level 1, maths Level 2, English Level 1, English Level 2, ICT Level 1, ICT level 2, NVQ, Btec, ERR, Apprenticeship Completion Certificate

(Not all qualifications are applicable for every course, check with your training provider for details of what certificates you could achieve during your course).

21 APPRENTICESHIP STANDARDS

The Apprenticeship Frameworks are now being slowly phased out. If you are already on an Apprenticeship Framework, then don't worry, the changes are not going to affect you.

The new Apprenticeship standards, have been developed by employer groups and these are known as 'trailblazers'.

The Apprenticeship standards will eventually take the place of the frameworks, but with so many qualifications on offer, it takes a long time to change from one system to another. The government have already discontinued some of the frameworks, but recently (2018) the government announced that they will not withdraw any further frameworks until 2020. By 2020 the government expect that all employers and providers will be ready to deliver the new qualifications.

What does this mean for you as an Apprentice?

The standards are said to be more robust and more suitable for industry. This is because they have been written by employer groups. This means that once you pass the Apprenticeship, you really should be very well trained in your chosen career subject.

It also means that you will need to have an End Point Assessment (EPA). You will need to pass an assessment at the end of your course, by an assessor who you have never met and who is completely impartial. You have to pass the EPA in order to complete your Apprenticeship course. Have a look at the section on EPA for further information.

Most standards have NO formal qualification as part of them. As a training provider, I found this hard to get my head around. Many training companies have chosen to build formal and nationally recognised qualifications into their Apprenticeship structure, but this is a choice, unlike with the old frameworks. So essentially there are less certificates on offer with the new standards, but you should get a more rounded qualification, which is more up to date and more suitable to the industry you are in.

Check with your training provider to see if they offer formal qualifications as part of their Apprenticeships. You will still work to get your maths and English functional skills if you need them, but the qualifications are no longer compulsory (for many of the standards) and many qualifications used to include ICT and do not any more. Once you have passed your EPA and Apprenticeship you will however receive a certificate of completion from the ESFA.

22 E-PORTFOLIO SYSTEMS AND PAPER FOLDERS

As you work through your Apprenticeship, you will need to complete a portfolio of evidence to show the work you have done, and to demonstrate your knowledge and competence levels.

There are an array of E-portfolio systems used by training providers to support your learning. Some training providers may still use paper portfolios. It doesn't matter which your centre use, but most now use E-portfolio for easier access, better reporting and tracking for the centre.

An E-portfolio may also be accessed at any time by you as the learner, your tutor, centre staff, the exam board or funding providers. In addition, your employer may be given access to your E-portfolio so that they can track your progress too.

The main E-portfolio systems are OneFile, Smart Assessor and Learning Assistant. All the systems are similar, and provide a range of supporting mechanisms to aid tracking of progression and learning.

The systems track the progress you have made so far on the course. By logging into your E-portfolio, you should be able to see your progress so far on your course, the evidence you have submitted, what work you have left to complete and tutor feedback on the work completed. You may also be able to see a 'lovely' picture of your personal tutor, internal verifier and employer as their accounts will be linked to yours. You should be able to send messages and feedback via the system to all of the same.

Some E-portfolio systems will give you access to resources, such as workbooks, study guides, video tutorials and links to websites. The system might give you access to reading lists relating to the course work you need to complete. In addition, there should be contact information available, which will allow you to contact the training provider, tutor and IV (the IV is the Internal Verifier who will approve your work prior to certification if applicable).

My personal preference for E-portfolio is OneFile, but that's pretty much all it is and most systems are robust and easy to use.

If you are given a choice of E-portfolio or paper folder, I would highly recommend E-portfolio. You can always print it out if you prefer paper - and using it might just help you improve your ICT skills. With E-portfolio you can access resources easily and see all your work beautifully displayed online. In addition, it means if you have a query, then authorised staff at the centre can access your account and help you out.

E-portfolio can't be lost, as the E-portfolio provider will have plenty of back-up systems in place, but a paper folder once lost, is lost - and if you leave it on the bus, then this could mean a year's worth of work, or more, might need to be re-written.

Ofsted encourage the use of ICT whenever possible. We are in the technological era and ICT skills are now a necessary part of the world of work in most industries. It's good to embrace it and learn new systems when you can as most of the skills you learn by using one system are often transferrable.

23 GATHERING EVIDENCE FOR YOUR PORTFOLIO

As you work through your Apprenticeship, you will need to produce evidence of your learning, skills and knowledge

If you are working towards a Btec or NVQ qualification, then you will need to show evidence for each element of the qualification and your tutor will support you to prepare this work.

As you develop your practical skills at work, you will be able to use evidence from the tasks you do in your day to day job.

For example, if you are working towards a Management Apprenticeship, you can hand in staff performance reviews, appraisals or meeting minutes that you have produced at work.

If you are working towards a Customer Service Apprenticeship, then you might have feedback from customer surveys that you could use, or emails to confirm that you have resolved a complaint for example.

You will need to show that you have the knowledge and understanding to meet the criteria for your qualification or Apprenticeship. This can be done by written assignments or the completion of workbooks. Some students have said that they don't want to do written assignments. Often evidence can also be obtained by voice recording or video, which can replace the need for written work.

Below is a list of ways of collecting evidence for your portfolio. This is not exhaustive, and some training providers/courses may have specific requirements.

- Written assignments
- Workbook completion
- Online tests
- Paper based tests
- Reflective accounts
- Witness statements
- Work-based product evidence (such as emails you've sent, your appraisal, samples of your work)
- Professional discussion
- Question and answer sessions recorded on voice recorder
- Video evidence
- Feedback from colleagues, managers, customers or peers
- Project work you may have completed

Normally training providers will ask you to show one piece of evidence to show your knowledge and understanding and two pieces of evidence to show your competence (or practical skills). This could vary depending on the quality of the evidence and the requirements of the training provider or examination board.

24 THE APPRENTICESHIP LEVY AND GOVERNMENT FUNDING

The Apprenticeship Levy came into force on 6th April 2017. This was a massive reform for Apprenticeship funding and basically means that large employers, rather than The Government, fund a lot of Apprenticeship courses.

Put briefly, any employer with a wage bill of £3 million or more a year (which is *very* roughly 120 employees), must pay into a "levy pot". The employer can then choose to pay to train and upskill existing staff (who then become Apprentices but retain existing benefits and pay etc.) or they can use the funds to take on new Apprentices.

Employers with a smaller wage bill still qualify for funding (subject to lots of rules), so the current system of taking on and funding courses still applies to them and is unaffected by The Levy.

As an Apprentice, how you are funded is not too much to worry about, as this should be looked after for you by the training provider. It is good to know how your course is funded though. Some private training providers sub-contract from colleges, so you may be able to benefit from their resources and support, such as Moodle accounts or other resources.

It is important to know if your Apprenticeship course has been paid by the Government or your employer.

I always explain to Apprentices that it is important to appreciate the opportunity they have. Funding for training may not always be there. You are very lucky to have this opportunity and you should make the most of it. If you look at the cost of privately funded qualifications you may understand how lucky you are to get a fully funded course, which will enhance your CV and, hopefully, enhance your career and thereby your long-term standard of living.

It's not all about money, but let's face it, the stronger your CV, the more money you are likely to earn. That means maybe a better house, car or holidays later in life. I find it very frustrating when Apprentices don't complete their course without good reason and give up important life chances. Not only that, but there is only so much funding to go around. If you waste funding then you might be taking an opportunity from someone else who may have made the most of it. I see it a bit like a hospital bed. If you weren't really sick then you wouldn't take the bed from someone who needed it would you?

I tell Apprentices at induction, that we want the most

enthusiastic, most committed learners who want to succeed. The Apprenticeship course is not compulsory, but a valuable opportunity that, in my opinion should not be wasted and should be respected for what it can bring to your career.

25 END POINT ASSESSMENT (EPA)

If you are on one of the new apprenticeship standard courses, you will be required to pass an End Point Assessment at the end of the course.

End point assessments are now here to stay, with the new standards becoming the future of Apprenticeships.

The Government is in the process of phasing out the old Apprenticeship Frameworks and phasing in the new Apprenticeship Standards. You should be told at induction (or prior) if the course you are on requires an End Point Assessment, as currently there are still many providers using the Apprenticeship Frameworks and many of the new Apprenticeship Standards have not yet been released.

The list of courses on the standards is being updated all the time so it is impossible to give you a comprehensive list of which courses require an End Point Assessment and which don't. So please make sure you ask.

A list of available standards is available however in Appendix 1, which is correct as of February 2018, but this is updated constantly as new courses are released.

Don't be put off if you are on one of the frameworks rather than the standards. You will not be losing out as both are equally valid and you will be given the opportunity to obtain suitable skills, knowledge and/or qualifications either way.

As you go through your course, you will work to produce evidence to show your knowledge and competence and most likely produce a portfolio of evidence (either on an E-portfolio or paper file) to show what you have achieved.

If your course requires an End Point Assessment (EPA) you will also need to prepare for this as well. The Government worked with employer groups to prepare the standards and so, the theory is, that the new standards will be more up to date and more in keeping with the needs of employers within your chosen industry.

The purpose of the End Point Assessment is to ensure that the Apprentice meets the standard set by employers and that they are then fully competent in their chosen occupation.

The End Point Assessment is a synoptic assessment of the knowledge, skills and behaviours that have been learnt throughout the Apprenticeship course. This test is taken at the end of the course when the employer, the training provider and you, the Apprentice, feel you are ready.

You will then enter the 'gateway' to take the assessment. End Point Assessments are graded by an independent assessor, who you will not have worked with previously, and works for an organisation other than your training provider or college.

End Point Assessment organisations must be on the Register of End Point Assessment Organisations and the organisation is normally chosen by your employer with support from your training organisation.

The End Point Assessment Organisation should work hard with you, to put you at ease to give you the best possible chance of passing. The end point assessments are generally graded, as pass, distinction or fail. Often there are 2 chances for re-assessment if you don't pass first time, but this will be costly to the employer or training provider, so they will do their best to make sure you are fully prepared prior to taking the test.

Once you have passed the end point assessment (EPA) you will receive a grade and then your certificate of achievement can be applied for by the EPA assessment organisation.

26 WHAT DOES THE END POINT ASSESSMENT INVOLVE?

Each Apprenticeship course has a written set of 'standards' which must be fully met in order to pass the End Point Assessment.

You should be able to obtain the standards from your personal tutor. They are all available online as well.

Have a look online for the standard and the assessment plan for the apprenticeship you are on. This will tell you exactly what you need to do to pass your EPA.

You may find that they are available to you in the resources section of your E-portfolio, or you may be given them during induction (or even before you take the job). It is important that you read these through and get to know what your End Point Assessor will be looking for. You can always search for them online if you're not given them.

End Point Assessments can vary, depending on the course you are on. Generally speaking, you will be required to take a multiple-choice test, a professional discussion (like an informal interview) and be observed working in your job role. You may be asked to showcase your portfolio of evidence or create a new 'mini portfolio' showcasing just specific evidence. All the EPAs are different and you will need to check on the assessment plan for your standard what you need to do.

Alternatively, you may be asked to submit a diary of work you have completed or a presentation to showcase your work to a panel of experts. The assessments chosen reflect the type of work you do and the course you are on, to show that you can cope in real-life situations and you have suitable knowledge and understanding to perform your role at the level you are working at.

27 ROLES AND RESPONSIBILITIES WITHIN APPRENTICESHIPS

The Employer

Your employer is there to support and train you for the duration of the Apprenticeship. Don't take this lightly though and think that the employer will put up with anything because they've contracted to support you for 12 months or more on an Apprenticeship. They can still discipline you, in the same way as other employees, they can also dismiss you or even make you redundant. Of course, they need to follow employment law, but an Apprentice is still a member of staff, and even if you are on minimum wage, they will want you to pull your weight and earn your money.

Your employer should however be supportive and support your training provider to give you the skills and knowledge you need to pass your Apprenticeship.

Your Personal Tutor

As an Apprentice you will normally be allocated a personal tutor. Your personal tutor will be responsible for ensuring that your work is to the right standard in order to ensure you are successful throughout the course. Your personal tutor will assess your work and give you feedback to help you to develop and enhance your skills and knowledge. A good personal tutor will stretch and challenge you to make you the best that you can be.

Your tutor/assessor is very important to you on your Apprenticeship journey. They are there to support you, talk to your employer, mark your work, resolve disputes if needed, teach you and give you feedback.

Your tutor will play a large part in your Apprenticeship success. They are *people*, please remember that. They do want to hear from you, but they do have a life themselves too. I have known students phone their tutor at 2am to ask a question, or even get their Dad to call them on a Sunday. This is not good behaviour. Email is best if you really need to contact your tutor out of office hours. You will find your tutor is also likely to decline friend requests on social media too, it's nothing personal, but they are obliged to keep a professional distance, even if you do work together so much that you feel like you are becoming friends.

The Internal Verifier (IV)

The Internal Verifier (or IV) is the person who works with your Personal Tutor to make sure your work meets the standards needed for the exam boards. The IV will check some, or all, of your work or they might even just make spot checks. Different centres will have their own rules about how much work an IV will check, this is called sampling.

When an IV samples your portfolio of evidence, they will check to see if the work you have submitted, that has been marked by your personal tutor, meets the standards claimed. If it does then great, the IV will mark it to state they have sampled it. If not then the IV will send it back to the personal tutor to ask them to make amendments, such as gather additional evidence or rectify administrative errors.

The IV will also be the person to approve your portfolio of evidence for sign off and completion. They may also be involved in supporting your tutor to prepare you for your End Point Assessment (EPA) if you are due to have one. In addition, the IV is a good point of call for you if you have any issues or complaints about your personal tutor. Many E-portfolio systems will show you who your IV is, and their details may also be documented in a paper portfolio. The IV is there to support your personal tutor, who in turn supports you.

The IV has a very important role in the centre. They make sure that standards are met so that the exam boards are happy with the quality of work done by learners. If the IV is doing a good job then when the exam boards come in to check the centre, there will be no issues.

You may have come across the term Internal Quality Assurer or IQA, which is an alternative name for an IV. The term IQA reflects the job description better as the IV job is to assure the quality of work produced by the centre staff, but as far as you need to know, they are pretty much the same thing.

The External Verifier or Standards Verifier

An External Verifier (EV), sometimes known as a Standards Verifier (SV), represent the exam boards. They come into centres periodically to check the standard of work produced by the centre meets their requirements.

An EV or SV will ask the centre to produce a sample of work for them to check and the centre will ensure this is prepared prior to the EV visit. The EV will be given guidelines on how many files to ask to see and they might also ask to see learner resources, such as workbooks or assignment briefs to check they support learners appropriately.

The EV or SV will interview a small sample of learners, either face to face or by telephone. If you do get a call from the EV or SV, don't worry, they are just doing their job and will most likely have chosen you at random. Ideally your personal tutor will call you first to explain that you have been selected to receive a call by the exam board and what to expect. The EV or SV will ask you questions such as:

- How are you finding the course?
- Do you feel you have been supported by your tutor?
- How did you choose your optional units? (if you have optional units that is)
- Have you been informed about the Appeals Procedure?

It is important that you be honest and tell the SV or EV your experiences. If you don't know an answer to a question, then don't worry, candidates often forget things they have been told (such as the Appeals Procedure) and the EV or SV will prompt you to try and remind you or to see if you at least know how to find the information, even if you don't remember the specific detail.

The EV will compile all the information required and then produce a report to show the standards attained by the centre. The EV supports centres to ensure work is to the standard it should be. Some exam boards also have a Lead Standards Verifier, who will come into centres and check their policies, procedures and working methods as well.

All this checking and verification is important for you as an Apprentice. Even though you may have no direct involvement in this, it is reassuring to know about, as it means that the qualifications you are working on are of a high standard and that they are respected by employers and nationally recognised.

28 INDUCTION AND GETTING STARTED ON YOUR COURSE

Once you have successfully obtained a place on an Apprenticeship course, you may be invited to attend a formal induction session. This could be a group session, held at a training centre or your place of work, or it could be a one to one session with your personal tutor.

The standard of induction training varies enormously between training providers. A good induction should include the following:

- An introduction to Apprenticeships
- A basic overview of the training provider and what they will offer you
- What you should expect of your training provider and what is expected of you as an Apprentice
- How long your course runs for
- Any additional benefits – such as discounted or free travel passes or discount cards
- What qualifications you will get at the end of the course
- If you will need to take an EPA (End Point Assessment)

- Where to obtain resources and reading material to support your learning
- In addition, you may also be asked to complete some work towards your NVQ/Btec as well as your Functional Skills – maths, English and ICT (as required).
- You may also get the opportunity to meet your personal tutor for the first time if you have not met him/her already

The induction process is important and whilst you may feel bombarded with information, it is essential that you use this opportunity to ensure that you are 100% committed to the course and the programme of study. Work will be the place where you spend the majority of your waking hours from now on, so you need to make sure that this is what you want to do and how you see your career moving forward.

Top tips for getting the most out of your induction session:

- Listen and make notes – even if no one else does
- Ask plenty of questions – you need to know what you are committing to
- Get a feel for the training provider and how they work
- Ask for a reading list if you have not been provided with one. A good basic book will help

you with your course work. It might be worth investing in buying one. There are lots of good books to support NVQ/Btec and Functional Skills online.

- Ask to see samples of the work of other students. Many centres will have anonymised examples for you to look at so that you get a good idea of the level of work expected of you
- Ask for a copy of the learner journey if the college or training provider have one. This will give you an idea of what you will go through at each stage of the course month by month
- Look around the centre or college – you will now be part of this learning environment. You need to feel happy that the centre and to feel that you will work well together

Remember – at induction it is not too late to back out of the course if you feel it is not right for you. It is better to back out at induction than six months in!

29 CENTRE APPEALS PROCEDURES

All training providers and colleges will have an Appeals Procedure or Appeals Process. This should be explained to you at induction or very early on in your Apprenticeship. The Appeals process should explain what you should do if you are unhappy with the marking process.

Appeals may be made against a range of issues relating to decisions made by the centre or their representatives, such as:

- Results of assessments – decisions made by the centre or by the EPA Centre
- An awarding body (ILM/Pearson or other awarding body that the learner is registered with) decision
- The centre or awarding body decision to decline a request for reasonable adjustment, special considerations, or the use of a language other than English, Welsh or Irish
- External Verifier's decision(s) in external quality assurance (EQA) of a Centre assessed learner work

All candidates have the right to challenge the assessment decision made by an assessor on a unit of competence. In addition, candidates have the right to challenge a functional skills final grade made by an awarding body.

There are specific terms and procedures outlined within the Appeals procedure documented by the centre. This may include things like – appeals must be made within 30 days or specific forms to be used. Some centres can charge a fee for appeals, but most will ask a senior member of staff to re-look at work and this can often be done informally. The appeals procedure should also explain what to do if you need to formalise a complaint beyond the centre.

You should have a good understanding of the appeals procedure, should you need it, and a copy should be made available to you. This could be published on the centre website or on your E-portfolio or paper portfolio.

30 CHOOSING A TRAINING PROVIDER

It is important to make sure that you have the right training provider. You will be working with this company or college for the entirety of your Apprenticeship – and maybe beyond, if you then move on to a higher-level Apprenticeship programme afterwards.

It is good to get a feel of the company/college. Even if you are offered a telephone interview only, it may be worthwhile to ask if you can come in and meet the staff and your potential personal tutor. Most centres should be happy for you to do this. If you are invited in for a face to face interview, use this as an opportunity to look around and get a feel for the training centre and meet some of the staff.

Normally you will deal with a Business Development Manager or Recruitment Consultant prior to starting your Apprenticeship. Make sure you get along with your consultant and ask as many questions as you can.

It is worth having a look at the training providers' website and social media pages. Company websites can give you useful basic information about the company such as how long it has been running and what courses are offered by that specific training company. Have a look to make sure the training provider offers a suitable selection of courses to suit your own needs. Many training providers will specialise in certain types of Apprenticeships (such as construction, business skills, hairdressing or health and social care).

In addition, have a look at social media. Looking at the training providers' Facebook page for example, will give you a good idea of their working methods and interests. For example, it is good to see that training providers celebrate the success of their learners through social media. This could be things such as running an Apprentice of the Month competition or posting photos of Apprentice success stories such as a promotion. You will also get an idea of extra-curricular activities the centre may be involved in, such as Anti-Bullying campaigns or charity fundraising events. Furthermore, centres may post information such as special offers for students, job opportunities or information to support the wider education of students, like Human Trafficking or Anti-Terrorism, or even important news articles.

The training centre you work with should have a good track record of success with students and should be able to provide evidence of it.

You may not get much choice about which training provider to work with however. This is because the training provider will have a contract with an employer and may be recruiting specifically for them. If that is the case, you should still do background checks on the centre to make sure you feel comfortable, but of course the job role and the right course may be your priority.

31 ROATP – REGISTER OF APPRENTICESHIP TRAINING PROVIDERS

The Register of Apprenticeship Training Providers gives details of organisations that are approved to deliver Apprenticeships. Any training provider or college delivering Apprenticeships must be listed on the RoATP.

For an organisation to be RoATP approved, they have been through a stringent application process with the ESFA (Education & Skills Funding Agency – the Government Organisation that pays for your Apprenticeship).

The ESFA check the company's financial health, capability to deliver Apprenticeships and quality of delivery. If you can't find your training provider on the RoATP don't panic, just check they don't use another trading name for their company or there may be another good reason. Really this is for employers and funders to check, not you as an Apprentice, but useful to know about.

RoATP Website:

https://www.gov.uk/guidance/register-of-apprenticeship-training-providers

The ESFA (Education and Skills Funding Agency) has given contracts to 714 Apprenticeship Training Providers for the period between January 2018 and March 2019. This gives you an idea of how many providers there are.

32 THE IMPORTANCE OF OFSTED REPORTS

Ofsted grade training providers in a similar way to schools and colleges.

Not all training providers will have had an Ofsted inspection, but if they have then it's worth having a look at the report before you start with a training provider. This will give you an insight into how they work and how successful they are.

Ofsted grade schools, colleges and training centres as below:

- OUTSTANDING
- GOOD
- REQUIRES IMPROVEMENT
- INADEQUATE

Ofsted reports are generally a very good indicator and a useful source of information when choosing a college or training provider. Ofsted will check that progression and outcomes for learners are effective and that the centre or college is well organised with quality teaching and learning strategies.

If you do have a look at the Ofsted report, don't just

look at the headline rating. You might find that a training provider has been marked as inadequate in one area, but has many other strengths in areas that are more applicable to your needs.

33 CHOOSING AN EMPLOYER

It is important to ensure that you chose an employer that suits you and your career ambitions. Make sure you check out your employer on the internet and social media if you can. You could also offer to spend a day, or a few hours, in the office or site to check that you like the working environment and to make sure it is for you. After all, you will be spending most of your waking hours there if you take on the job.

Employers from all types take on Apprentices, from small family run firms, to multi-national corporations. The Top 100 Apprenticeship Employers from the National Apprenticeship Service shows the range of opportunities available with employers.

Check out your potential employers' website and social media pages to get a good idea of how they work and what they offer to their clients or customers.

34 FUNCTIONAL SKILLS

Functional skills have been a mandatory component of apprenticeships since October 2012 and even though there has been a recent reshuffling of qualifications and a greater emphasis on GCSEs within apprenticeships, functional skills will remain a fundamental aspect of apprenticeships for the foreseeable future.

Most Apprenticeship courses require learners to take maths, English (and possibly ICT) functional skills qualifications.

The majority of courses require maths and English only, courses such as Team Leading Level 2 and Business Administration Level 2 and 3 also require ICT.

For learners on a level 2 course the minimum requirement is to pass Level 1 Functional Skills (and to at least work towards level 2) and for level 3 and above most courses require Level 2 Functional Skills.

Apprentices who already have GCSE or O'Level grade C or above are exempt from Functional Skills. Specific courses will have specific requirements and you will need to check if your previous qualifications meet the requirements.

Functional skills help lay the foundation for a great career. You cannot pass your Apprenticeship without passing your functional skills or having equivalent qualifications. If your course requires an EPA (end-point assessment) then you will not be allowed to take the EPA until you have passed your functional skills or given in evidence that you have equivalent qualifications.

35 EXAMPLES OF FUNCTIONAL SKILLS REQUIREMENTS

Apprenticeship Course	Functional Skills Requirement	Additional comments
Management Level 4 Apprenticeship Framework	There is no Functional Skills Requirement for this course	Learners are encouraged to show progression even though there is no formal test
Bricklaying Level 2 Apprenticeship Framework	Maths and English Level 1	Learners should progress to level 2 whenever possible
Business Administration Level 2 Apprenticeship Framework	Maths, English and ICT Level 1	Learners should progress to level 2 whenever possible
Customer Service Practitioner Level 2 (standard)	Maths and English Level 1 pass and at least take examinations for level 2	Learners should progress to level 2 whenever possible
Warehouse and Storage Level 2 Apprenticeship Framework	Maths, English and ICT Level 1	Learners should progress to level 2 whenever possible
Operations/Departmental Manager Level 5 (standard)	Maths and English Level 2	There is no ICT requirement

Always check the Functional Skills requirements for your course with your training provider

Your personal tutor should be able to provide you with plenty of support and training to help support you to pass your Functional Skills examinations.

Many centres have a dedicated Functional Skills teacher, who will provide additional teaching and learning sessions for Apprentices who need these qualifications. The Functional Skills teacher will support learners by providing group and/or one to one sessions.

Some Functional Skills teachers will go to the workplace to deliver training, which can help with the cost and time involved in travelling to the training centre.

Some training centres will insist on day release to the centre. This very much depends on what course you are on and the structure offered by the centre. This is something that should be made clear to you during induction and if you are unsure of the process then please ask plenty of questions.

36 WHAT HAPPENS IF I FAIL MY FUNCTIONAL SKILLS TESTS?

To fully pass your Apprenticeship course, you will need to pass your Functional Skills tests to the required level. However, you can re-sit your Functional Skills examinations. You may need extra support sessions from your Functional Skills Tutor or Personal Tutor to achieve this. This can normally be arranged by talking to your Personal Tutor.

Centres often monitor their 'first time pass rates' for Functional Skills. This means that they will want you to pass – as a good first-time pass rate indicates good levels of teaching and learning. Ofsted examiners may look at centre's first-time pass rates. It is important for centres to ensure you are as ready as you can be, prior to putting you in for your test.

Again, I think a lot of this is down to effort by you as a student. If you are given all the tools you need to help you succeed, then you should be set up for success.

The upshot here is, that if you don't study hard then

realistically you might not pass.

This isn't school though and Functional Skills are quite different to GCSEs. Maths especially is quite different to GCSE, in that Functional Skills Maths looks more at practical application of mathematical skills, meaning that it makes more sense to students. A typical Maths Level 1 question might ask you to look at how many fence panels you might need around a garden or how much paint you'd need to cover certain sized walls. Another example would be using supermarket special offers, such as comparing 3 for the price of two items, or percentage discounts on clothing. These are practical mathematical concepts which most students seem to relate to well.

Many students tell me that maths is especially what scares them. When I explain that it is so different from maths at school, Apprentices do seem more open to studying maths again in order to improve their skills and knowledge.

Anyway, I digress, so we were looking at what happens if you don't pass your Functional Skills tests.

As I explained above, you can re-sit. A question I often get asked is 'how many times can I re-sit?' This is essentially up to the centre or college to agree. I have had one student who re-sat her maths test four times. This wasn't because she couldn't do the maths calculations, but more to do with her stressing out as soon as she sat in the examination room. This is where the skills of your personal tutor come in. In this case, we agreed to take the test to her work. She sat the test in her own office. This was of course conducted with full exam conditions, but in an environment where she felt more comfortable and at ease.

It is important that you speak to your tutor if you have any concerns. If you don't feel ready for the test on the date your tutor sets, then explain this to them.

You might be panicking about nothing, and as I said, your tutor wants you to pass first time, so they won't want to rush you into tests you are not ready for. If you have learning difficulties or special needs, then you need to let your tutor know. They may be able to arrange for extra time for your exams, or even for a reader to be with you during the test.

Most centres will try to get you to take your Functional Skills exams within the first six months of your course. This should give you then plenty of time for re-sits if needed or other help to support you to pass.

It is worth noting that recent legislation has come into effect which changes the minimum English and maths requirements needed to complete an Apprenticeship for people with a learning difficulty or disability. The changes will lower the English and maths requirements for these apprentices to an Entry Level 3 qualification, you will need to check with your training provider or college to see if this is applicable for you as conditions apply.

If you have done all you possibly can and still have not passed your Functional Skills by the end of your Apprenticeship, then you will not achieve full completion. However, many courses have several elements to the Apprenticeship, such as Btec or NVQ qualifications, so, as long as you complete these, you could still walk away with great qualifications to enhance your CV, and don't forget all that experience and employer support you have gained whilst on the course.

37 ELECTRONIC SUPPORT FOR FUNCTIONAL SKILLS TEST PREPARATION

Many centres will offer online resource material or learning platforms to help you with your self-study in preparation for your exam.

Popular resource platforms include BKSB or ForSkills. Centres will decide which learning platform they use and will direct you accordingly and provide you with a user-ID and password for access.

These systems are very effective at developing your skills in these areas. Systems such as BKSB and ForSkills ask learners to complete a "Diagnostic Assessment". This is where the system analyses your strengths and weaknesses. This is an excellent tool, as it will help you by giving you activities and resources that meet your own personal needs, so you do not waste time working on areas you are already competent at.

These systems are costly to the centres. Centres often pay, per learner, to access. This means they will want to see you working hard on your course work for Functional Skills.

Often these systems integrate with the E-portfolio you will be using, so that your personal tutor can keep an eye on your progress and provide support when needed.

You should keep evidence of the work you do towards your Functional Skills exams, as your tutor will require this. Tutors may give you tasks to complete that support your Functional Skills while working towards your Btec or NVQ at the same time. For example, a learner working on a Business Administration qualification may be asked to produce a spreadsheet to show the productivity of co-workers. This could then cover, maths, ICT and make progress towards his or her Btec or NVQ units at the same time. This holistic assessment method works well to make sure that learners work is time-effective and productive, whilst enhancing real-life work skills simultaneously.

The more you use the system the more you will get out of it, and therefore the more likely you are to pass your exams.

38 FUNCTIONAL SKILLS EXAMINATIONS

Functional Skills Examinations consist of the following:

Maths – A formal examination – normally done on a computer or laptop. Some centres offer paper based examinations but most are now completed electronically. It is very important to show working out when taking this examination. Results normally take up to 30 days, but can often be much quicker.

English – Separate Reading and Writing Examinations, normally taken at the training centre or your place of work. In addition, there will be a Speaking and Listening Assessment. Results normally take up to 30 days, but can often be much quicker.

The Speaking and Listening Assessment can be conducted at your place of work or at the training centre. You will be required to take part in designated activities to show your communication and preparation skills. You should be advised at the end of the session if you have passed or not, or shortly afterwards.

ICT – This is completed electronically. Candidates are required to complete a practical activity, such as making a flyer or poster, usually based on a work-related scenario. This normally includes internet research, completion of a spread-sheet with formulas or functions, creation of a graph or chart and sending a mock email. In addition, there may be some questions about e-safety, viruses or handling system issues. This examination normally takes 2 hours. Results normally take up to 30 days. ICT results tend to take longer to come through than maths and English results.

You can find past papers for Functional Skills online. The link below will take you to Pearson past papers and should give you an idea of what level of understanding is expected of you when you take your tests, but be aware your training centre may not use this exam board so it may be a good idea to find out who they use and look at past papers specific to your course.

http://qualifications.pearson.com/en/support/support-topics/exams/past-papers.html

39 NATIONAL APPRENTICESHIP WEEK

National Apprenticeship Week is held at the beginning of March each year. It is coordinated by the National Apprenticeship Service and is designed to celebrate Apprenticeships.

The idea is to promote Apprenticeships and the positive impact they have on the economy, businesses and individuals.

During National Apprenticeship Week, employers and Apprentices join together to celebrate and showcase the success of Apprentices across England.

This event promotes the benefits of Apprenticeships to potential candidates as well as employers and can help people to understand the value of Apprenticeships as a viable and worthwhile career option.

The National Apprenticeship Service (NAS) is part of the Education and Skills Funding Agency, who coordinate and promote the delivery of Apprenticeships in England.

Below is a list of useful websites for you to refer to, which will give you more information about National Apprenticeship Week.

https://www.gov.uk/government/topical-events/national-apprenticeship-week-2017

https://www.fenews.co.uk/press-releases/15062-national-apprenticeship-week-2018

https://www.gov.uk/government/topical-events/national-apprenticeship-week-2018-naw-2018

https://nawevents.co.uk/

40 CASE STUDY EXAMPLES: TYPICAL STUDENT EXPERIENCES

Case study 1 – Lilly

Lilly was only 16 when she began her Apprenticeship. Lilly wanted to work in an office, so she applied for a Business Administration Level 2 Apprenticeship.

Lilly applied for several roles and was initially unsuccessful. She spent time improving her CV and practising her interview technique. She was eventually offered a role within a large building company, within their head office.

Lilly was taken under the wing of the Head of Department, who supported her in her job role and gave her additional tasks to stretch and challenge her. Lilly completed her Business Administration Apprenticeship at level 2 and was offered a place on a level 3 Apprenticeship. Lilly was offered the opportunity to do accountancy qualifications by her employer and she chose to do these qualifications first and then she went on to complete her Level 3 Business Administration Apprenticeship.

Lilly has since been promoted and taken on much more responsibility. She even organised a fund raiser for her company as part of a project she was given and she raised over £5000 for the charity. She is highly thought of by her employer who said that "she is an asset to the company and we would not be without her".

Case Study 2 – Josh

Josh was already in a job when he heard about the Apprenticeship Scheme. He was working for a large call centre in Birmingham as a Team Leader.

Josh wanted to obtain a formal qualification and so he enrolled on a Team Leading Level 2 Apprenticeship. This helped to support Josh's knowledge and understanding and helped him to gain ideas about team work, team development and how to make teams successful and hit targets.

Josh completed his Team Leading Level 2 Apprenticeship successfully.

Having been a model student, Josh was offered a Level 3 Management Apprenticeship and a very decent pay rise from his employer.

Josh was also promoted by his company and given a role training new staff, as well as management of a small group of team leaders.

He continued his work on his Apprenticeship and completed his course successfully. He has now gone on to complete a Level 4 Management Apprenticeship, and is now considering a Level 5 Operations/Departmental Management Apprenticeship. His employer has supported him throughout and he stayed with the same training provider. He was nominated for Btec Apprentice of the Year and got through to the final rounds, although he didn't win!

case study names have been changed for confidentiality purposes, but are based on real-life learners and their experiences

41 YOUR APPRENTICESHIP JOURNEY

Your journey as an Apprentice should provide you with the skills, knowledge and experience to begin, or build upon, the best possible career opportunities available to you.

As a potential Apprentice, or someone who is supporting an apprentice, it is important to arm yourself with as much information as you can to support you in making well thought through career choices.

Have high expectations, not only of your training provider and employer, but of yourself too. This is **your** journey. BE THE BEST YOU CAN BE and don't look at what others have achieved or strive for, but look at self-improvement and self-development.

By learning from those around you and gaining nationally recognised qualifications, working hard and maintaining a positive attitude, your career prospects are unlimited, and Apprenticeship opportunities provide an excellent starting point.

Have a look at the websites listed in the next

section as these will give you further information and guidance. Well done, you are making positive steps by researching information about careers.

42 USEFUL WEBSITES FOR FURTHER INFORMATION

ACAS Employment Rights Helpline
http://www.acas.org.uk/index.aspx?articleid=4489

All about school leavers
https://www.allaboutschoolleavers.co.uk/articles/article/235/how-to-find-a-list-of-all-the-apprenticeships-available

Amazing Apprenticeships
https://twitter.com/AmazingAppsUK

Apprenticeship Helpline
Nationalhelpdesk@apprenticeships.gov.uk or Telephone 0800 015 0400

Apprenticeships in Wales
http://gov.wales/topics/educationandskills/skillsandtraining/apprenticeships/?lang=en

BKSB Functional Skills Online Training
https://www.bksb.co.uk/

ESFA
https://www.gov.uk/government/organisations/educ

ation-and-skills-funding-agency

ForSkills Functional Skills Online Training
http://www.forskills.co.uk/

Further Education and Skills Apprenticeships
https://www.gov.uk/topic/further-education-skills/apprenticeships

Get in, Go Far Government Apprenticeship Website
https://www.getingofar.gov.uk/

National Apprenticeship Service
https://www.gov.uk/apply-apprenticeship

Pearson Past Papers for Functional Skills
http://qualifications.pearson.com/en/support/support-topics/exams/past-papers.html

Register of Apprenticeship Training Providers
https://www.gov.uk/guidance/register-of-apprenticeship-training-providers

Removal of Apprenticeship Frameworks
https://www.gov.uk/government/publications/removal-of-apprenticeship-frameworks

The Apprenticeship Centre Facebook Page
https://www.facebook.com/TheApprenticeshipCentreBirmingham/

The Apprenticeship Centre
http://www.apprenticeship-centre.co.uk/

The Apprenticeship Levy

https://www.gov.uk/government/publications/apprenticeship-levy-how-it-will-work/apprenticeship-levy-how-it-will-work

The Ask Project

https://amazingapprenticeships.com/

The Institute for Apprenticeships

https://www.instituteforapprenticeships.org/

If you feel you are not quite ready for an Apprenticeship, but would like training in a new career, you could try a Traineeship. For details see https://www.gov.uk/find-traineeship

43 ABOUT THE AUTHOR

Louise Webber studied Psychology and Philosophy at The University of Liverpool. She then went on to study Management at Postgraduate Level. Louise worked for three major banking institutions at management level and was very successful at meeting targets and audit requirements.

Louise went on to work in the education sector, working in both mainstream and special needs schools. She then re-trained to work within the adult education sector and studied to become a tutor/assessor for NVQ and Apprenticeships as well as becoming a Lead Internal Verifier within a training centre. Louise currently works within the centre as Head of Apprenticeships, responsible for the success of the Apprenticeship schemes, staff training and development, recruitment and quality management. Louise is also the Ofsted nominee for the centre.

Louise has supported her team of tutors to successfully complete over 2000 Apprenticeship/NVQ courses for learners within the training centre where she works. In addition, Louise has worked as a Standards Verifier for the world's largest examination board, supporting other centres to achieve high standards for learners and success within the education sector.

Elizabeth Thomas

Editor

44 ACKNOWLEDGEMENTS

I would like to thank my loving family and friends for all their support and the fantastic colleagues and friends I have at The Apprenticeship Centre, who strive to ensure all learners succeed and develop within their Apprenticeship courses.

Finally, I dedicate this book to my lovely daughters who brighten my life each and every day.

45 DISCLAIMER

Every effort has been made to ensure the currency, validity and accuracy of information contained within this book, however the publisher, author and editor cannot be held responsible for any errors or omissions, however caused. No responsibility for loss or damage occasioned by any person acting or otherwise, as a result of information contained within this book can be accepted by the author, editor or publisher. This book was published independently of The Apprenticeship Centre and associated businesses. Centre processes may vary.

46 FIRST PUBLISHING DATE

This book was first published in February 2018.

Copyright: 2018 Louise Webber

47 APPENDIX 1: LIST OF APPRENTICESHIP STANDARDS AVAILABLE (FEB 18)

Control / technical support engineer (degree)

Electrical / electronic technical support engineer (degree)

Financial services administrator

Installation electrician / maintenance electrician

Manufacturing engineer (degree)

Network engineer

Power network craftsperson

Product design and development engineer (degree)

Relationship manager (banking)

Software developer

Laboratory technician

Science manufacturing technician

Food and drink maintenance engineer

Actuarial technician

Dental technician

Dental laboratory assistant

Dental practice manager

Golf greenkeeper

Junior journalist

Property maintenance operative

Railway engineering design technician

Digital and technology solutions professional (degree)

Dual fuel smart meter installer

Water process technician

Financial services customer adviser

Investment operations administrator

Investment operations specialist

Senior financial services customer adviser

Workplace pensions (administrator or consultant)

Investment operations technician

Able seafarer (deck)

Nuclear welding inspection technician

Public service operational delivery officer

Aerospace engineer (degree)

Aerospace software development engineer (degree)

Conveyancing technician

Licensed conveyancer

Chartered legal executive

Paralegal

Solicitor

Laboratory scientist

Science industry maintenance technician

Nuclear health physics monitor

Nuclear scientist and nuclear engineer (degree)

Paraplanner

Refrigeration air conditioning and heat pump engineering technician

Chartered surveyor (degree)

Surveying technician

Systems engineering masters level

Utilities engineering technician

Butcher

Chartered manager (degree)

Gas network craftsperson

Gas network team leader

Motor vehicle service and maintenance technician (light vehicle)

Insurance practitioner

Dental nurse

Mortgage adviser

Insurance professional

Housing / property management assistant

Senior housing / property management

Non-destructive testing engineering technician

Junior energy manager

Land-based service engineer

Land-based service engineering technician

Live event rigger

Bespoke tailor and cutter

Public sector commercial professional

Gas engineering

Outside broadcasting engineer (degree)

Boatbuilder

Credit controller / collector

Digital marketer

Cyber intrusion analyst

Data analyst

Unified communications trouble shooter

Infrastructure technician

Junior management consultant

Junior 2D artist (visual effects)

Assistant technical director (visual effects)

Aviation ground specialist

Aviation ground operative

Rail engineering advanced technician

Rail engineering technician

Rail engineering operative

Software tester

Engineering design and draughts person

Commis chef

Welding - level 2

Welding - level 3

Hospitality team member

Cyber security technologist

Healthcare science assistant

Transport planning technician

Retailer

Healthcare assistant practitioner

Healthcare support worker

Operations / departmental manager

Team leader / supervisor

Papermaker

Embedded electronic systems design and development engineer

HM Forces serviceperson (public services)

Supply chain operator

Large goods vehicle (LGV) driver

Supply chain warehouse operative

Broadcast production assistant

Aircraft maintenance certifying engineer

Survival equipment fitter

Professional accounting taxation technician

Lead adult care worker

Travel consultant

Airside operator

Customer service practitioner

Aviation operations manager

Highways electrician / service operative

Highway electrical maintenance and installation operative

Fire emergency and security systems technician
Electrical power protection & plant commissioning
engineer

Associate project manager

Food and drink advanced process operator

Food and drink process operator

Food technologist

Non-destructive testing (NDT) operator

Assistant accountant

Bus and coach engineering technician

Heavy vehicle service and maintenance technician

Road transport engineering manager

Furniture manufacturer

Hospitality supervisor

Senior chef production cooking

Retail team leader

Aviation maintenance mechanic (military)

IT technical salesperson

Compliance / risk officer

Senior compliance / risk specialist

Sports turf operative

Maintenance and operations engineering technician

Retail manager

Advanced credit controller / debt collection specialist

Advanced dairy technologist

Healthcare science associate

Senior healthcare support worker

Advanced butcher

Financial Adviser

Software Development Technician

Unified Communications Technician

Associate Ambulance Practitioner

Hair Professional

Spectacle Maker

Event Assistant

Composites Technician

Power Engineer (degree)

Facilities Management Supervisor

Nuclear Technician

Building Services Engineering Installer

IS Business Analyst

Postgraduate Engineer (Degree)

Healthcare Science Practitioner (Degree)

Chef De Partie

Registered Nurse (degree)

Steel Fixer

Fishmonger

Building Services Engineering Craftsperson

Junior Content Producer

Mineral Processing Mobile and Static Plant Operator

Accident Repair Technician

Baker

Building Services Design Technician

Animal Technologist

Arborist

Horticulture and Landscape Operative

Forest Operative

Bespoke Saddler

Food Industry Technical Professional (degree)

Building Services Engineering Ductwork Craftsperson

Project Controls Technician

Metrology Technician

Rail Infrastructure Operator

Passenger Transport Driver - bus coach and rail

HR Consultant / Partner

HR Support

Building Services Engineering Ductwork Installer

Building Services Engineering Service and Maintenance Engineer

Building Services Engineering Ventilation Hygiene

Digital Engineering Technician

Business Administrator

Housing/property management

Adult care worker

Building services design engineer (degree)

Civil engineer (Degree)

Civil engineering technician

Organ builder

Engineering technician

Engineering construction pipefitter

Process automation engineer (degree)

Teacher

Accountancy / taxation professional

Senior insurance professional

Advanced Manufacturing Fitter

Air Traffic Controller

Animal Care and Welfare Assistant

Animal Trainer

Animator (Degree)

Archaeological Technician

Architect (Degree)

Architectural Assistant (Degree)

Asbestos Analyst/Surveyor

Asbestos Removal Operative

Autocare Technician

Automotive Engine Test Engineer (decommissioned)

Automotive Glazing Technician

Automotive Industry Customer Service Advisor (decommissioned)

Bid and Proposal Co-ordinator

Blacksmith

Book keeper

Bookbinder

Brewer

Broadcast and Communications Engineer

Broadcast and Communications Principal tech

Broadcast & Communications Technical

Broadcast and Communications Technician

Building Services Engineering Site Management (degree)

Building Services Engineering Technician

Business Fire Safety Advisor

Business to Business Sales Professional (Degree)

Cabin Crew

Career Development Professional

Caster

Castings Foundry & Patternmaking Operative

Castings Foundry & Patternmaking Technician

Ceramic Mould Maker Operative

Chartered Town Planner (Degree)

Children Young People & Families Manager

Children Young People & Families Practitioner

Civil Engineering Site Management (degree)

Cleaning and Support Services Operative

Clinical Coder

Clinical Dental Technician

Clinical Trials Specialist (degree)

clock maker

Commercial Airline Pilot

Community Activator Coach

Community Arts Co-ordinator (Cultural Learning/Participation Officer)

Community Coordinator/Associate Community Manager

Community Energy Specialist

Community Safety Advisor

Community Sport and Health Officer

Construction and Civil Engineering Ground Worker

Construction Assembly Technician

Construction Design and Build Technician

Construction Design Management (degree)

Construction Quantity Surveyor (degree)

Construction Site Engineering Technician

Construction Site Management

Construction Site Supervisor

Construction Surveying Technician

Countryside worker

Creative Venue Technician

Crop Technician

Cultural Heritage Conservation Technician

Custody & Detention Officer

Customer Service Specialist

Cyber Security Technical Professional (Degree)

Data scientist (degree)

Decorator

Demolition Operative

Dietitian (degree)

Digital and Technology Solution Specialist

Digital applications technician

Digital User Experience (UX) Professional

Early Years Lead Practitioner (degree)

Early Years Senior Practitioner

Ecologist (degree)
Electrical Power Networks Engineer
 [previously Power Networks Engineer]
Electrical Electronic Product/Service &
/Installation Engineer

Emergency Service Contact Handling

Engineering Construction Erector/Rigger

Environmental Manager (degree)

Equine groom (horse care)
European Refrigeration Air Conditioning
and Heat Pump Design & Applications Engineer

Express delivery Manager (Degree)

Express Delivery Operative

Fabricator

Facilities Management (Degree)

Facilities Manager

Facilities Services Operative

Fall Protection Technician

Farrier

Fashion Studio Assistant

Fencing Installer

Financial Services Professional

Firing Operative

Fitted Interiors and Multi Skilled Maintenance Operative

Floorlayer

Floristry

Food and Drink Advanced Engineer (Degree)

Food and Drink Manufacturing Manager (Degree)

Fork Lift Truck Technician

Formworker

Funeral Director

Funeral Team Member

Further Education Assessor/Coach

Further Education Learning and Skills Teacher

Further Education Learning Mentor

Garment/Product Technologist

Geospatial Mapping and Science (Degree)

Geospatial Survey Technician

Glass Manufacturing Operator

Glazing Operative

Golf Course Manager

Hand engraver

Hearing Aid Dispenser

Heritage Carpenter and Joiner

Heritage Engineering Technician

High Speed Rail & Infrastructure Technician

Highways Maintenance Skilled Operative

Highways Maintenance Supervisor

Hospitality Manager

Improvement Specialist

Improvement Practitioner

Improvement Technician

In Situ Flooring

Industrial Coatings Applicator

Intelligence Analyst

Interior Systems

Internal Audit Practitioner

International Freight Forwarding Specialist

IT solution technician

IT Support (decommissioned)

Jewellery Maker

Journeyman Bookbinder

Junior Estate Agent

Landscape/Horticulture Supervisor

Lead Practitioner in Adult Care

Leader/Manager in Adult Care

Learning and development consultant

Learning and development practitioner

Leather Craftsperson

Leisure & Entertainment Engineering Technician

Leisure Duty Manager

Leisure Team Member

Lift/Escalator Electromechanic

Lifting Technician

Live Event Technician

Local Government Revenues and Benefits Officer

Locksmith

Mammography Assistant Practitioner

Lean Manufacturing Operative

Manufacturing Technology Engineer (degree)

Marinas and Boatyard Operative

Marine Engineer

Marine Pilot

Maritime Caterer

Maritime Operations Officer

Marketing Executive

Marketing Manager

Master Builder with a major in bricklaying (Bricklayer)

Master Builder with a major in plastering (Plasterer)

Metal Decking Installer

Metal Recycling General Operative

Military Construction Engineering Technician

Maritime Electrical / Mechanical Mechanic

Mineral and Construction Product Sampling and Testing Operations

Mineral Processing and Static Plant Engineer

Mineral Processing Weighbridge Operator

Mineral Products Technician

Minister In Pastoral Charge (Degree)

Modeller

Motor Finance Specialist

Motorcycle Technician (repair and maintenance)

Museums & Galleries Technician

Network Cable Installer

Network Operations

Nuclear Operative

Nursing Associate

Occupational Therapist (Degree)

Operating Department Practitioner (degree)

Operational Firefighter

Optical Assistant

Oral Health Practitioner

Outdoor Sports

Packhouse Team Leader

Painter and Decorator

Paramedic (degree)

Passenger Transport onboard & station team member

Passenger Transport Operations Manager

Pattern Cutter

Payroll administrator

Personal Trainer

Pest Control Technician

Pharmacy services assistant

Pharmacy Technician

Photographer

Physicians Associate (Degree)

Physiotherapist (degree)

Piling Attendant

Plant Hire Desk Controller

Plumbing and Domestic Heating Technician

Podiatrist (Degree)
Police Community Support Officer
Police Constable (degree)
Policy Officer
Port Agent
Port Marine Operations Officer
Port operative
Port Plant machinery Operative
Poultry Technician
Poultry Worker
Powered Pedestrian Door Installer and Service Engineer
Print Finisher Prepress Operative & Printer
Probate Technician
Process Control Systems Engineer (degree)
Production Chef
Production Manager (Degree)
Professional Economist (degree)
Professional Internal Auditor
Props Technician
Propulsion Technician
Prosthetics and Orthotics (degree)
Psychological Wellbeing Practitioner
Public Relations Assistant
Public Relations Consultant (degree)
Publishing Assistant
Puppet Maker
Rail & Rail Systems Principal Engineer (Degree)
Rail & Rail Systems Senior Engineer (Degree)
Recruitment Consultant
Recruitment Resourcer
Registrar
Regulatory Affairs Specialist (degree)
Regulatory Compliance Officer
Rehabilitation Practitioner
Rehabilitation Worker (Visual Impairment)
Resource Operative
Resource Technical Manager

Retail Management (degree)

Risk and Safety Management Professional (Degree)

Roofer

Safety Health and Environment Technician

Sales Executive

Scaffolder

School Business Professional

Science Industry Process/Plant Engineer (Degree)

Science Manufacturing Process Operative

Security First Line Manager

Selector

Senior Chef Culinary Arts

Senior Equine Groom

Senior Hair Professional

Senior Investment/Commercial Banking Professional

Senior Metrology Technician

Serious and Complex Crime Investigator (Degree)

Sewing Machinist

Shoemaker

Slip Preparation Operative

Small business financial administrator

Smart Home Technician

Social Worker (Degree)

Sonographer (degree)

Specialist Rescue Operative

Specialist Textile Technician

Specialist Tyre Operative

Sporting Excellence Professional

Stairlift Platform Lift Service Lift Electromechanic

Steeplejack

Stockperson (beef pigs sheep dairy)

Stonemason

Storyboard Artist (Degree)

Structural Steelwork Erector

Structural Steelwork Fabricator

Supply Chain Leadership Professional (degree)

Supply Chain Practitioner (Fast Moving Consumer Good)

Teaching Assistant

Technician Scientist

Temporary Traffic Management Operative

Textile Care Operative

Textile Manufacturing Operative

Thermal Insulation Operative

Thermal Insulation Technician

Trade Supplier

Tunnelling operative

Underkeeper

Vehicle Damage Assessor (degree)

Vehicle Damage Mechanical Electrical and Trim (MET) technician

Vehicle Damage Paint Technician

Vehicle Damage Panel Technician

Veterinary Nurse

Video Games Quality Assurance Technician

Voluntary and Community Sector Worker

Wall and Floor Tiler

Watchmaker

water treatment operative

water treatment technician

Ordnance Munitions and Explosives (OME) Professional (degree)

Wireless Rigging Technician

Wood Product Manufacturing

Workboat Crewmember

Youth Worker

Improvement Leader

Carpentry and Joinery

Digital Marketer (Degree)

Beauty Professional

Abattoir Worker

Academic Professional (Degree)

Accounts Assistant

Acoustics Technician

Actuary

Advanced Baker

Advanced Beauty Professional

Advanced Carpentry and Joinery

Advanced Clinical Practitioner (degree)

Advanced Golf Greenkeeper

Journalist (degree)

Engineering operative

Non-Destructive Testing Engineer (degree)

Degree Apprenticeship Speech/Language Therapist

Diagnostic Radiographer (degree)

Therapeutic Radiographer (degree)

Boatmaster Tidal Inland Waterways

Cycle mechanic

Marine Technical Superintendent (degree)

Food and Drink Engineer

Creative Digital Designer Degree Apprenticeship

Senior Leader Master's Degree Apprenticeship (Degree)

Project Manager Integrated Degree Apprenticeship

Laboratory scientist (Degree)

Early Years Educator

Rail & Rail Systems Engineer

Ambulance support worker

Commercial Procurement and Supply
BEMS (Building Energy Management Systems)
Controls Engineer

Packaging professional

To check for the most up to date information on available Apprenticeship standards go to
https://www.gov.uk/government/publications/apprenticeship-standards-list-of-occupations-available--2

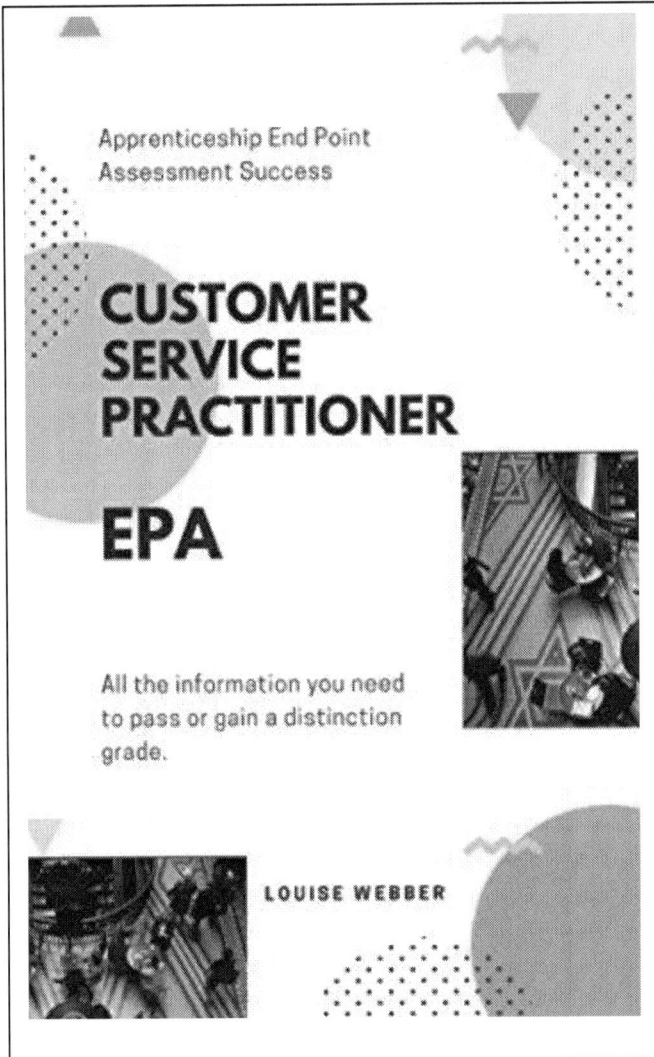

Apprenticeship End Point Assessment Success

CUSTOMER SERVICE PRACTITIONER

EPA

All the information you need to pass or gain a distinction grade.

LOUISE WEBBER

Also available on Amazon by Louise Webber.

Printed in Great Britain
by Amazon

43678707R00077